Mr. Book

STEVE HAWKES

PAGE PUBLISHING, INC.
New York, NY

First originally published by Page Publishing, Inc. 2019

ISBN 978-1-64544-306-3 (Paperback)
ISBN 978-1-64544-307-0 (Digital)

Printed in the United States of America

There was a little house out in the country…
much like many others,
but
yet so unique.

However, the inside of this house was very unusual,
From its owners to its walls and floors.

Books... Books were everywhere... They were in the living room, the bedroom, and even the kitchen.

Oh, yes, the owner…

His name is Herbert Longfellow Book.

That's right, Book, and yes, he loved them more than anything.

Herbert moved out to the country so he could read and live in total silence.

Like being in a very quiet library.

Sssssss…

Herbert's quiet life was about the same, day after day. He wrote articles for a newspaper and sent them off to an office far away, and he got more and more boxes of books till he almost had too many. Was it possible?

Herbert's life was about to change. He was asked to write an article about ten local public libraries in the state that were closing down due to the fact that no one wanted to read from books anymore.

Herbert simply looked down at his cats, Seuss and Osborne, and said to them,

"Well, I guess there will be more books for me.

"So? Who cares?"

Then the very next morning, a new box of books arrived. Herbert walked slowly around his home; there was no place to put them.

Herbert decided to go to sleep. Maybe he'll have a good idea when he wakes up. *Yes, I'll sleep on it*, he thought. He had an amazing dream that he was piloting a giant book, dropping books for kids to read as he flew across the countryside.

The next day, he heard a soft knock on the door. Herbert froze; he slowly walked to the door and opened it even slower. There was a small note on his steps. It read:

Dear Mr Book, can I Broow a Book about a Queen.

Love
mia ps
thank you

Someone loved me and wanted a book to read. Herbert's heart felt different; it felt well…"happy."

Herbert immediately began looking for the right book for Mia.

Mmmm, *The Story of the Happy Queen*, perfect. He placed the book on his front steps.

It wasn't long before more kids were leaving notes and not just Mia. Ethan and Susan asked for books on the American Revolution. "Sure, I can help with that," Mr. Book said to himself.

His world wasn't so small anymore.

In the meantime, Herbert discovered he was outgrowing his home. He could barely move anymore. He had to do something.

He suddenly felt sad. How could he leave his wonderful books? How could he keep his job of writing and lending out books to kids?

He looked out his window, and down at the end of his quiet street was an old broken-down RV. It looked rough, but then Herbert felt a moment of relief and excitement.

He would need to work fast.

Herbert read many books about repairing RV engines and how to fix up RV interiors. Before long, it was ready.

Ready for its new purpose.

Ready to be filled with what?

Books, of course.

He would travel to small towns to give out books to kids and to adults too. Books about many things.

His world was no longer small but much bigger now.

Preliminary Sketch

Interior Plans
Mr Books - Mobile.
HLB.ü B H L B

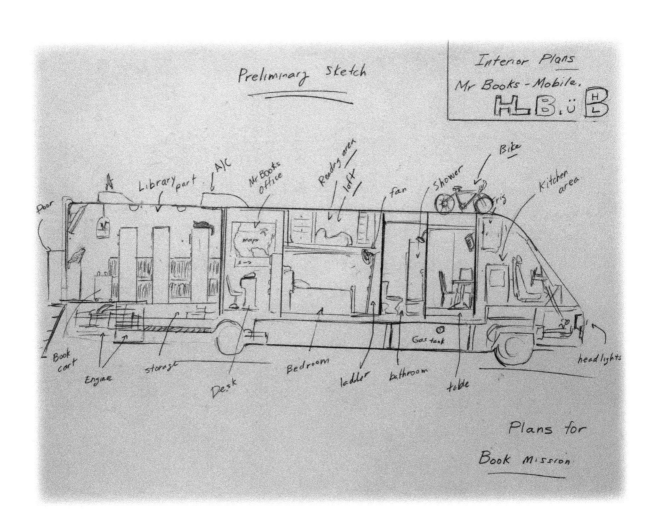

Door
Library part
A/C
Mr Books Office
Reading area
loft
fan
Shower
Bike
frig
Kitchen area
Maps
Book cart
Engine
storage
Desk
Bedroom
ladder
bathroom
Gas tank
table
headlights

Plans for
Book Mission

33

Herbert even turned part of the RV into his bedroom and small kitchen area. He, of course, took Seuss and Osborne and the two birds that became part of the family.

He had a mission in mind.

Herbert had a new life to share with others about what he loved and was good at. It brought his life new meaning and a new purpose, and now new roads opened in front of him.

As he was driving, Mr. Book thought to himself, *I do care now.*

And he felt good inside.

Mr. Book's three rules:

1. Care for others (pets and people).
2. Share your talents and the things you love.
3. Look outside the small worlds we live in; you just might find new friends and new roads to follow.

About the Author

Steve Hawkes (illustrator and author) lives in Bethlehem, Pennsylvania, with his wife, Zuzana, and two kids, Mia and Ethan. By day, he is a school social worker who works with special-needs students, and by night a dad, husband, brother, artist, craftsman, history lover, ice hockey coach, and comedian (maybe). He is excited to publish his first book that was a three-year process of artwork and development. He plans more books in the future. He hopes this book will serve to help children stay more connected to one another in a world which seems to be more detached. Visit a library and keep reading!

CPSIA information can be obtained
at www.ICGtesting.com
Printed in the USA
BVHW091137031219
565406BV00007B/139/P

9 781645 443063